Hacked Justice: The Chronicles of AJ, The White Hat Hacker From Philly

Prologue: The Beginning of the End

Philadelphia has always been a city of contrasts. The historical charm of Old City, the gritty realism of South Philly, the vibrant energy of Center City – it's a place where the past and present collide in a chaotic dance. For someone like me, AJ, it's the perfect playground.

By day, I blend into the crowd, just another face in the sea of humanity. By night, I become a ghost in the machine, a phantom navigating the intricate web of cyberspace.

Hacking isn't just a skill; it's an art, a way of life. It started as a hobby in high school, something to pass the time between classes. But it quickly became an obsession, a means to escape the mundane reality of everyday life.

My apartment, a modest one-bedroom in Fishtown, is a testament to my dual existence. On the surface, it looks like any other living space – a couch, a coffee table, a kitchen cluttered with takeout containers. But in the corner of the room, hidden behind a folding screen, is my sanctuary.

Multiple monitors display lines of code, surveillance feeds, and encrypted communications. It's here that I feel most alive, most in control.

It was a typical Tuesday night when everything changed. I was in the middle of a particularly challenging hack, attempting to breach the security of a high-profile financial institution.

The thrill of the chase, the adrenaline rush – it was intoxicating. But just as I was about to crack the final layer of encryption, my screen went black. Panic surged through me. This wasn't a normal glitch.

Before I could react, the screen flickered back to life, displaying a single message: "We need to talk. FBI."

My heart raced. I'd always known the risks, the possibility that one day the authorities would catch up with me. But seeing those three letters on my screen made it all too real. I considered running, disappearing into the digital abyss. But curiosity got the better of me. I typed a response, my fingers trembling slightly.

"Who is this?"

A moment later, another message appeared. "Agent Sarah Carter. We need your help."

Help? The FBI needed my help? It sounded like a trap, but something in the tone of the message intrigued me. Against my better judgment, I agreed to meet.

The rendezvous point was a small café in Center City, a place I frequented often enough to blend in but not so much that I'd be recognized.

I arrived early, scanning the crowd for any signs of danger. Then I saw her – a woman in her early thirties, dressed in a sharp suit, her eyes scanning the room with a mixture of caution and determination. She spotted me and gave a slight nod.

I took a deep breath and approached her table. "Agent Carter?"

She smiled, though it didn't reach her eyes. "AJ, I presume. Thank you for coming."

We exchanged pleasantries, but it was clear she wasn't here for small talk. She got straight to the point. "We have a situation, and we believe you're the only one who can help us."

I raised an eyebrow. "And why would I do that?"

Her expression hardened. "Because if you don't, you'll be spending the next few decades behind bars."

The threat hung in the air between us. I knew she wasn't bluffing. But there was something else, a hint of desperation in her eyes. This wasn't just about catching a hacker. There was more to the story.

"Alright," I said finally. "Tell me what you need."

And that was the beginning of the end. The moment that set everything in motion. Little did I know, it would be a journey that would test my skills, my morals, and my very identity.

Chapter 1: The Call

I couldn't shake the feeling of unease as I left the café. Agent Carter had given me just enough information to pique my interest but not enough to fully understand the scope of the situation.

She'd mentioned a series of high-profile cyber crimes, each more sophisticated than the last, and a criminal mastermind known only as "Specter." It sounded like something out of a movie, but the seriousness in her eyes told me this was very real.

Back in my apartment, I fired up my computer and began digging. Specter was a ghost in the digital world, leaving no trace of their true identity. But their handiwork was evident – data breaches, financial scams, ransomware attacks. They were meticulous, calculated, and seemingly unstoppable.

The more I delved into Specter's activities, the more I realized the scale of the threat. This wasn't just about money or information; it was about power and control.

Specter's targets were influential figures, major corporations, and even government agencies. The implications were staggering.

It was clear why the FBI was desperate, but why involve me? There were plenty of skilled hackers out there, some even working within the agency. I couldn't shake the feeling that there was something they weren't telling me.

Just as I was about to call it a night, my phone buzzed. It was a message from Agent Carter.

"Tomorrow. 10 AM. Same place."

No pleasantries, no explanation. Just a time and place. I sighed, knowing I didn't have much of a choice. If I wanted answers, I had to play along.

The next morning, I arrived at the café a few minutes early. Agent Carter was already there, nursing a cup of coffee and looking over some documents. She glanced up as I approached and motioned for me to sit.

"Morning," I said, trying to sound casual.

She nodded. "Good morning. I appreciate you coming."

"Do I have a choice?"

A hint of a smile tugged at her lips. "Fair point. Let's get down to business."

She handed me a file, and I began to flip through it. Detailed reports on Specter's known activities, profiles of suspected associates, and a list of potential targets. It was overwhelming, to say the least.

"We believe Specter is planning something big," Carter said, her tone serious. "Something that could cause widespread chaos. We need to stop them before it's too late."

I looked up from the file. "And you think I can help because...?"

"Because you're one of the best," she replied without hesitation. "And because you know how to think like them."

Her words sent a chill down my spine. She wasn't wrong. I'd spent years honing my skills, learning to navigate the darkest corners of the internet. But that didn't mean I wanted to be on the other side of the law.

"What's in it for me?" I asked, leaning back in my chair.

"A clean slate," she said simply. "Help us take down Specter, and your past indiscretions will be forgiven."

It was a tempting offer, one that I couldn't easily refuse. But there was still a nagging doubt in the back of my mind.

"And if I say no?"

Carter's expression hardened. "Then we'll have no choice but to pursue legal action against you. And believe me, we have enough evidence to put you away for a long time."

I sighed, knowing she had me backed into a corner. "Fine. I'll do it. But I want full access to your resources and complete transparency. No more secrets."

She nodded. "Agreed. Welcome to the team, AJ."

As I left the café, I couldn't help but wonder what I'd just gotten myself into. The path ahead was uncertain, and the stakes were higher than anything I'd ever faced. But one thing was clear – there was no turning back now.

Chapter 2: The Decision

The days that followed my meeting with Agent Carter were a blur of conflicting emotions. Part of me was excited by the challenge, the chance to pit my skills against one of the most notorious hackers in the world.

But another part of me was terrified. What if I couldn't pull it off? What if Specter was too smart, too elusive?

My doubts weighed heavily on me as I returned to my apartment, my sanctuary. I sat in front of my array of monitors, staring at the blank screens. This was my domain, the place where I felt most in control. But now, the weight of the task ahead made it feel like a prison.

I needed to clear my head, so I grabbed my jacket and headed out for a walk. The streets of Philadelphia were bustling with life, people going about their daily routines, oblivious to the digital war happening behind the scenes.

As I walked, my mind wandered back to the early days of my hacking career.

I remembered the thrill of my first successful hack, the rush of adrenaline as I bypassed security protocols and accessed forbidden data. Back then, it was all about proving myself, about pushing the limits of what was possible. But over time, it became more than that. It became a way to challenge the system, to fight back against the powers that be.

But now, I was being asked to switch sides, to use my skills to uphold the law instead of breaking it. The irony wasn't lost on me.

As I wandered through the city, I found myself drawn to a small park I used to visit as a kid. It was a place of solace, a refuge from the chaos of my childhood. I sat on a bench, watching the world go by, and thought about the choices that had led me here.

I could walk away, disappear into the shadows and live a life on the run. Or I could stay and face the challenge head-on, knowing that failure wasn't an option. The more I thought about it, the clearer it became. This was my chance to make a difference, to use my talents for something greater than myself.

By the time I returned to my apartment, my mind was made up. I would help the FBI take down Specter, no matter the cost. But I would do it on my terms, using my methods.

I spent the next few days preparing, gathering the tools and resources I would need for the task ahead. I reached out to a few trusted contacts in the hacking community, seeking their advice and support. Most were skeptical, some outright hostile to the idea of working with the feds. But a few understood the stakes and offered their assistance.

One of those contacts was an old friend named Max, a brilliant coder with a knack for finding hidden vulnerabilities.

Max and I had worked together on several projects over the years, and I knew I could trust him.

"You're playing a dangerous game, AJ," Max said during a late-night call. "But if anyone can pull it off, it's you."

"Thanks, Max. I appreciate the vote of confidence," I replied, feeling a surge of determination.

"Just be careful, alright? Specter is no joke. And the FBI... well, let's just say they have their own agenda."

"I know. I'll watch my back."

With Max's support and the FBI's resources, I felt more confident in my decision. But there was still one person I needed to talk to, someone who had been a mentor to me in the early days of my hacking career.

I made my way to a small, unassuming bookstore in a quiet part of town. The owner, a grizzled old man named Henry, had a reputation as one of the best hackers in the business back in his day.

He'd retired from the digital world years ago, but he still kept his ear to the ground.

Henry greeted me with a knowing smile as I entered the store. "AJ, it's been a while. What brings you here?"

"I need your advice, Henry," I said, cutting straight to the point. "I've been approached by the FBI. They want me to help them take down Specter."

Henry's eyes widened in surprise. "Specter? That's a tall order. What's in it for you?"

"A clean slate. And the chance to do some good."

Henry nodded thoughtfully. "It's a risky move, but it sounds like you've thought it through. Just remember, the FBI isn't always as straightforward as they seem. Keep your wits about you."

"I will. Thanks, Henry."

As I left the bookstore, I felt a sense of resolve settle over me. I had the support of my peers, the wisdom of my mentor, and the determination to see this through. It was time to face the challenge head-on.

The next morning, I met with Agent Carter and her team at the FBI's Philadelphia field office. The building was a stark contrast to the chaotic world of hacking – all clean lines and polished surfaces. Carter introduced me to the team, a mix of seasoned agents and tech experts.

One of the key members was a tech specialist named Mike, a wiry guy with glasses and a quick wit. He would be my main point of contact within the FBI, helping me navigate their systems and resources.

"Welcome to the team, AJ," Mike said with a smile. "We've got a lot of work ahead of us."

I nodded, feeling a mix of excitement and apprehension. "Let's get started."

Over the next few weeks, we dove headfirst into the mission. I spent hours poring over data, analyzing Specter's patterns, and devising strategies to counter their moves. The work was intense and often frustrating, but there was a sense of purpose that kept me going.

One night, as I was working late in the FBI's secure lab, Mike walked in with a look of concern. "We've got a problem," he said, handing me a folder.

I opened it and scanned the contents. It was a report detailing a recent cyber attack on a major financial institution. The methods used were eerily similar to Specter's previous attacks, but there was something different, something more sophisticated.

"This isn't Specter," I said, frowning. "It's someone else, someone new."

Mike nodded. "That's what we think too. Specter may have a copycat, or worse, an accomplice."

The revelation added a new layer of complexity to our mission. Not only did we have to track down Specter, but we also had to identify and neutralize this new threat. It was a daunting task, but I was determined to see it through.

As the weeks turned into months, the pressure mounted. There were moments of doubt, moments when I questioned whether we would ever catch Specter. But there were also moments of triumph, small victories that kept us going.

One of those victories came in the form of a breakthrough. I'd been analyzing a series of encrypted messages intercepted from Specter's network when I noticed a pattern. It was subtle, almost imperceptible, but it was there – a hidden code within the encryption.

I spent hours deciphering the code, my fingers flying over the keyboard as I pieced together the puzzle. Finally, the message became clear. It was a location, a warehouse in the industrial district.

I immediately alerted Agent Carter and the team. We moved quickly, coordinating with local law enforcement to stage a raid on the warehouse. The operation was tense, every second feeling like an eternity.

As we breached the building, we were met with resistance. Specter's associates were well-prepared, and a fierce firefight ensued. I stayed back, monitoring the situation from a safe distance, my heart pounding in my chest.

Finally, the gunfire ceased, and the team secured the area. Among the captured was a key associate of Specter, a hacker known as Razor. He was a slippery character, but we managed to bring him in for questioning.

In the interrogation room, Razor was defiant at first, refusing to cooperate. But as the hours wore on, the weight of his situation became apparent. He knew the game was up.

"You think you've won?" Razor sneered. "Specter is just the beginning. There are others out there, more powerful than you can imagine."

His words sent a chill down my spine. We had made progress, but the battle was far from over. The digital war raged on, and the stakes were higher than ever.

As I left the interrogation room, Agent Carter approached me. "Good work, AJ. We've made a dent, but we need to keep pushing. Specter won't go down without a fight."

I nodded, my resolve stronger than ever. "I won't stop until we take them down. Whatever it takes."

The path ahead was uncertain, filled with danger and challenges. But I was ready to face it, to use my skills to bring justice to the digital world. And as long as I had the support of my team, I knew we could succeed.

The decision had been made. There was no turning back now. The fight against Specter had only just begun.

Chapter 3: Into the Web

With Razor in custody and a significant breakthrough under our belts, the momentum of the investigation shifted. We had a foothold in Specter's network, but it was just the beginning. Every piece of information Razor provided was like a puzzle piece, slowly revealing the bigger picture.

Back in the lab, I began to dive deeper into the web of connections.

Specter's network was vast and intricate, a labyrinth of false identities, encrypted communications, and hidden servers. It was clear that whoever Specter was, they were a master of their craft.

Days turned into nights as I poured over the data, rarely leaving the secure confines of the FBI's tech lab. Mike was a constant presence, his sharp mind and quick thinking invaluable. We developed a rhythm, a silent understanding of each other's strengths and weaknesses.

One evening, as I was decoding a particularly challenging set of files, Mike pulled up a chair next to me. "I've been thinking," he said, his eyes scanning the lines of code on my screen. "We need to understand Specter's endgame. What's their ultimate goal?"

I leaned back, rubbing my temples. "Power, control, chaos? It's hard to say. But whatever it is, it's big. They're not just a hacker; they're orchestrating something on a massive scale."

Mike nodded, his expression thoughtful. "We need to get ahead of them, anticipate their moves. And for that, we need to get inside their head."

It was a daunting task, but he was right. To catch Specter, we had to think like Specter. I turned back to my screen, my mind racing with possibilities.

As I continued to work, I decided to reach out to some old contacts in the hacking community.

These were people I'd known for years, some friends, some rivals, but all of them respected my skills. If anyone had information on Specter, it would be them.

One of those contacts was a hacker known as "Echo." Echo was a legend in the underground hacking scene, a ghost who could slip in and out of systems without leaving a trace. We'd worked together on a few projects in the past, and I knew I could trust them.

After a few hours of encrypted messages and secure communications, Echo agreed to meet. The rendezvous was set in a dingy bar on the outskirts of the city, a place where privacy was a given and questions were never asked.

I arrived early, scanning the dimly lit room for any signs of trouble. Echo was already there, a hooded figure hunched over a laptop in the corner. I approached cautiously, taking a seat opposite them.

"Echo," I said quietly.

They looked up, their face partially obscured by the hood. "AJ. Long time."

I nodded. "I need your help. I'm working with the FBI to take down Specter."

Echo's eyes widened in surprise. "The FBI? You've gone straight?"

"Something like that," I replied with a wry smile. "Specter is a threat to everyone, Echo. We need to stop them."

Echo was silent for a moment, considering my words. Finally, they nodded. "Alright. What do you need?"

"Information," I said. "Anything you know about Specter. Associates, methods, targets. We need to get inside their network."

Echo leaned back, their fingers tapping rhythmically on the table. "Specter is a ghost, AJ. But there are whispers, rumors. I've heard of a group called the Black Hat Syndicate.

They're a shadow organization, and Specter might be connected to them."

It was a lead, the first real one we'd had. "Tell me more."

Echo shared what they knew, bits and pieces of information that painted a picture of a highly organized and secretive group. The Black Hat Syndicate was involved in everything from cyber espionage to financial crimes, and they had connections in high places.

"Be careful, AJ," Echo warned. "These people are dangerous. They won't hesitate to eliminate anyone who gets in their way."

"I will," I promised. "Thanks, Echo."

As I left the bar, my mind was racing. The Black Hat Syndicate was a formidable adversary, but it was also a potential weakness. If we could infiltrate their network, we might be able to uncover Specter's identity and plans.

Back at the lab, I shared the information with Mike and Agent Carter. We began to formulate a plan, a multi-pronged approach to infiltrate the Black Hat Syndicate and gather intelligence on Specter.

The first step was to identify key members of the Syndicate. Using the data from Echo and Razor, we created a list of potential targets. It was a mix of hackers, financiers, and middlemen – each playing a crucial role in the Syndicate's operations.

One name stood out among the rest – a hacker known as "Viper." Viper was a notorious figure in the hacking world, known for their ruthlessness and cunning. If anyone had direct connections to Specter, it would be Viper.

We decided to focus our efforts on tracking down Viper. It was easier said than done. Viper was a ghost, constantly on the move, always one step ahead of the authorities. But everyone has a weakness, and it was my job to find Viper's.

Days turned into weeks as we worked tirelessly to locate Viper. I used every trick in the book, leveraging my contacts, analyzing data, and running complex algorithms to predict Viper's movements. It was a game of cat and mouse, and the stakes couldn't be higher.

Finally, we caught a break. A series of digital breadcrumbs led us to a small, unassuming house in the suburbs. It was the last place anyone would expect to find a notorious hacker, which made it the perfect hiding spot.

We coordinated with local law enforcement to stage a raid. The operation was tense, every second feeling like an eternity. But in the end, it was a success. Viper was taken into custody, their equipment seized for analysis.

In the interrogation room, Viper was defiant at first, refusing to cooperate. But as the hours wore on, they began to crack. The realization that their network was compromised, their associates captured, and their anonymity shattered was a heavy blow.

"I'll talk," Viper finally said, their voice filled with resignation. "But I want protection."

Agent Carter leaned forward, her expression stern. "You'll get protection, but only if you give us everything you know about Specter and the Black Hat Syndicate."

Viper nodded, defeated. "Alright. I'll tell you everything."

The information Viper provided was a treasure trove. Detailed accounts of the Syndicate's operations, key figures, and most importantly, Specter's role within the organization. Specter wasn't just a hacker; they were a puppet master, pulling the strings from behind the scenes.

But there was one piece of information that stood out above the rest – Specter's real identity. Viper didn't know the full name, but they had a lead – an alias, "Phantom," and a location, an old warehouse in the industrial district.

It was the break we'd been waiting for. We began to plan the next phase of the operation, a coordinated effort to track down Phantom and uncover Specter's true identity.

As the pieces of the puzzle began to fall into place, I couldn't shake the feeling that we were getting closer to the endgame. The digital war was reaching its climax, and the stakes were higher than ever.

But one thing was clear – we were not alone. The Black Hat Syndicate was vast and powerful, and they wouldn't go down without a fight. The path ahead was filled with danger and uncertainty, but I was ready to face it.

With the support of the FBI and my friends in the hacking community, I knew we could succeed. The battle against Specter was far from over, but we were closer than ever to uncovering the truth.

The hunt for Phantom had begun, and there was no turning back now.

Chapter 4: First Strike

The plan to capture Phantom was set into motion with precision. Every detail was meticulously thought out, every potential outcome considered.

The warehouse in the industrial district was our target, and we had to move quickly to avoid tipping off Specter or the Black Hat Syndicate.

Agent Carter and Mike coordinated with local law enforcement and federal agents to ensure we had the manpower and resources needed for the operation. It was a high-risk mission, and failure was not an option.

On the night of the raid, I found myself in a van parked a few blocks away from the warehouse, monitoring the situation through a secure feed. My heart raced as I watched the live video streams from the agents' body cameras.

This was it – the moment we had been working towards for months.

Agent Carter's voice crackled through my earpiece. "All units, move in."

The team moved with military precision, breaching the warehouse with a combination of speed and stealth. The initial entry was met with little resistance, but as they pushed deeper into the building, the true nature of the Syndicate's operations became apparent.

Rows of servers and computer equipment filled the space, each one meticulously maintained and humming with activity. This was more than just a hideout – it was a nerve center for Specter's network.

As the agents secured the area, I focused on the digital side of the operation. Using the feeds from the agents' cameras, I began to map out the network, identifying key points of interest and potential vulnerabilities.

"AJ, we've got something," Mike's voice came through the comms. "A secured room in the back. Looks like it could be Phantom's command center."

"Roger that," I replied, my fingers flying over the keyboard. "I'm accessing the security system now."

The feed from the secured room came to life on my screen. Inside, a figure was hunched over a computer, their face obscured by a hood. This had to be Phantom.

"Phantom is in the secured room," I relayed to the team. "Proceed with caution."

The agents moved in, breaching the door with practiced ease. Phantom barely had time to react before they were subdued and taken into custody. The operation had been a success, but there was still work to be done.

As Phantom was escorted out of the warehouse, I focused on extracting as much data as possible from their computers.

This was a goldmine of information – emails, transaction records, encrypted communications.

It would take time to sort through it all, but I knew there were valuable insights to be found.

Back at the lab, I worked late into the night, sifting through the data. Mike and Agent Carter joined me, their presence a reminder of the stakes. We were closer than ever to uncovering Specter's true identity, but there was still much we didn't know.

"Phantom was careful," I said, my eyes scanning the lines of code on the screen. "They used multiple layers of encryption, but there's something here. A pattern."

Mike leaned over my shoulder, studying the screen. "What kind of pattern?"

"It's a series of timestamps and locations," I explained. "Meetings, drop points, transactions. If we can decode it, we might be able to trace it back to Specter."

Agent Carter nodded. "Do whatever it takes, AJ. We're running out of time."

I worked through the night, my mind focused on the task at hand. The pattern slowly began to take shape, revealing a web of connections that spanned the globe. Each piece of information brought us one step closer to Specter.

By morning, I had compiled a list of key locations and potential targets.

It was a roadmap of Specter's operations, and it gave us the edge we needed.

"We've got them," I said, a sense of satisfaction washing over me. "This is the key to taking down Specter."

Agent Carter and Mike looked over the list, their expressions a mix of determination and anticipation. "Good work, AJ," Carter said. "We'll start coordinating with our international counterparts. This ends now."

The next phase of the operation was a coordinated effort to dismantle Specter's network. It involved multiple agencies, each one targeting a specific aspect of the Syndicate's operations. It was a massive undertaking, but it was our best chance to bring Specter to justice.

As the operation unfolded, I continued to monitor the situation from the lab. It was a delicate balance, coordinating with agents on the ground while maintaining the digital front. Every move had to be precise, every decision calculated.

There were moments of tension, moments when it seemed like the operation might fall apart. But each time, we managed to pull through, our determination unwavering.

One of the key targets was a financial hub in Europe, a place where Specter laundered money and conducted transactions. The local authorities had been tipped off, and a team of agents was dispatched to raid the facility.

As I watched the live feed from the raid, my heart pounded in my chest. The agents moved in, securing the area and confiscating evidence. It was another victory, another step closer to our goal.

But the most crucial part of the operation was still to come – capturing Specter. The data we had gathered pointed to a remote location in South America, a secluded compound hidden in the jungle. It was the heart of Specter's operations, the place where they directed their global network.

The team prepared for the final raid, knowing that this was the moment of truth. Agent Carter and Mike would be leading the charge, and I would be coordinating from the lab.

As the team moved in, the tension was palpable. The compound was heavily fortified, and the element of surprise was crucial. The agents breached the perimeter, moving swiftly and silently.

Inside the compound, the resistance was fierce. Specter's associates fought back with everything they had, but the agents were relentless. As the battle raged on, I focused on disabling the compound's security systems, giving our team the upper hand.

Finally, they reached the central command room. The door was breached, and inside, they found Specter – a figure hunched over a computer, frantically trying to erase evidence.

"Hands up!" Agent Carter shouted, her weapon trained on Specter.

Specter turned, their face a mask of defiance. "You think you've won? This is just the beginning."

But the fight was over. Specter was taken into custody, and the compound was secured. The digital war had reached its climax, and we had emerged victorious.

Back at the lab, the sense of relief was overwhelming. We had done it – we had taken down Specter and dismantled the Black Hat Syndicate. It was a victory for justice, a triumph of determination and skill.

As I sat back in my chair, the exhaustion finally catching up with me, I couldn't help but feel a sense of pride. We had faced impossible odds and come out on top. But the journey was far from over.

There were still questions to be answered, still loose ends to tie up. But for now, we could celebrate our victory, knowing that we had made a difference.

The first strike had been a success, but the battle for justice was far from over.

Chapter 5: The Trap

The capture of Specter was a major victory, but as we soon discovered, it was only the beginning. The data we had recovered from the compound revealed the full extent of Specter's network, and it was more extensive and far-reaching than we had ever imagined.

Specter had been operating under multiple aliases, each one managing a different aspect of their global operations.

While we had captured the central figure, there were still numerous associates and sub-networks that needed to be dismantled.

In the days following the raid, Agent Carter and I worked tirelessly to analyze the data and map out the remaining elements of Specter's network. It was a massive undertaking, but with each piece of information, we got closer to understanding the full scope of their operations.

One of the most critical pieces of information we uncovered was the existence of a secondary command center, a fallback location that Specter had set up in case of emergencies. This command center was located in a remote part of Eastern Europe, and it was heavily fortified.

"We need to take this place down," Agent Carter said, her eyes fixed on the map displayed on the screen. "If we don't, Specter's associates will regroup and continue their operations."

I nodded in agreement. "But we need to be smart about it. We can't just storm in like we did with the compound. This place is a fortress."

"We need a trap," Mike added, his expression thoughtful. "Something to lure them out and catch them off guard."

The idea was risky, but it was our best chance. We began to formulate a plan, one that involved using the information we had gathered to set a trap for Specter's remaining associates.

It would require careful coordination and precise execution, but if it worked, it would cripple their operations once and for all.

The first step was to create a false sense of security. We planted misinformation, making it seem like the FBI was moving on to other targets and that the command center was no longer a priority. It was a delicate balance, but our deception paid off.

Over the next few weeks, we monitored the command center closely, watching as activity began to pick up. Specter's associates, thinking they were safe, started to regroup and resume their operations.

With the trap set, we prepared for the next phase of the operation. This time, we needed a different approach – one that involved stealth and subterfuge rather than brute force.

We assembled a specialized team of agents trained in covert operations. Their mission was to infiltrate the command center, gather intelligence, and disable key systems to pave the way for the main assault.

As the team moved in, I monitored their progress from the lab, my heart pounding in my chest. The tension was palpable, every second feeling like an eternity. But the team was highly skilled, and they moved with precision and stealth.

Inside the command center, the team planted devices to disable the security systems and gathered crucial intelligence on the remaining associates. It was a dangerous mission, but their training and expertise paid off.

With the command center's defenses weakened, the main assault team moved in. The element of surprise was on our side, and the resistance was minimal. One by one, Specter's associates were captured, and the command center was secured.

As the operation came to a close, the sense of relief was overwhelming. We had successfully dismantled the heart of Specter's network, and their operations were crippled.

Back at the lab, we began to analyze the data recovered from the command center. It was a treasure trove of information, revealing the full extent of Specter's operations and their connections to other criminal organizations.

But there was one piece of information that stood out – a series of encrypted messages that suggested Specter had a contingency plan, one that involved a massive cyber attack on a global scale.

"We need to stop this," Agent Carter said, her expression grim. "If these messages are accurate, Specter's final act could cause unprecedented chaos."

We worked around the clock to decipher the messages and understand the full scope of the planned attack.

It was a race against time, but we were determined to prevent it.

As we dug deeper, we uncovered a plot to target critical infrastructure in major cities around the world. The attack was scheduled to take place in a matter of days, and the consequences would be catastrophic.

"We need to act fast," I said, my mind racing with possibilities. "We can't let this happen."

Agent Carter nodded. "We need to coordinate with our international counterparts and prepare for a global response. This is bigger than any of us."

The next few days were a whirlwind of activity as we worked to prevent the attack. We shared our findings with agencies around the world, coordinating a massive effort to secure critical infrastructure and neutralize the threat.

It was an unprecedented operation, one that required cooperation and coordination on a global scale. But as the clock ticked down, we managed to thwart the attack, averting what could have been a global catastrophe.

In the aftermath, the full extent of Specter's network was revealed, and their associates were brought to justice. It was a hard-fought victory, but it was a victory nonetheless.

As I sat back in my chair, the exhaustion finally catching up with me, I couldn't help but feel a sense of pride. We had faced impossible odds and come out on top. But more importantly, we had made a difference.

The trap had worked, and Specter's network was dismantled. But the fight for justice was never truly over. There would always be new threats, new challenges to face.

But for now, we could celebrate our victory, knowing that we had done what was right. And as long as there were people willing to stand up and fight for justice, there was hope.

The battle against Specter was over, but the war against cybercrime would continue. And I was ready to face whatever came next.

Chapter 6: Allies and Enemies

The successful dismantling of Specter's network was a major milestone, but it also marked the beginning of a new chapter in our fight against cybercrime. The intelligence we had gathered revealed the existence of numerous other criminal organizations operating in the shadows, each one as dangerous and elusive as Specter.

In the aftermath of the operation, we began to regroup and reassess our strategy.

The fight against cybercrime was far from over, and we needed to be prepared for whatever came next.

One of the first steps was to consolidate our resources and strengthen our alliances. The cooperation and coordination with international agencies had been crucial in thwarting Specter's final attack, and it was clear that a united front was our best defense against future threats.

Agent Carter and Mike spearheaded the effort to build a global network of allies. We reached out to law enforcement agencies, intelligence communities, and private sector partners, sharing our knowledge and expertise to create a collaborative force against cybercrime.

But as we forged new alliances, we also encountered new enemies. The dismantling of Specter's network had created a power vacuum, and other criminal organizations were quick to seize the opportunity.

One of those organizations was known as "The Shadow Collective." They were a group of highly skilled hackers and cybercriminals, and their goal was to establish dominance in the digital underworld. Their methods were ruthless, and they showed no hesitation in targeting anyone who stood in their way.

The Shadow Collective quickly became our primary adversary, and it was clear that they were a formidable opponent.

Their attacks were precise and coordinated, often targeting critical infrastructure and high-profile individuals.

To combat this new threat, we needed to gather as much intelligence as possible. I began to reach out to my contacts in the hacking community, seeking information on the Shadow Collective and their operations.

One of those contacts was a hacker known as "Vortex." Vortex was a well-known figure in the underground hacking scene, and while we had never worked together directly, I knew of their reputation as a skilled and resourceful hacker.

After several encrypted messages and secure communications, Vortex agreed to meet. The rendezvous was set in a secluded park on the outskirts of the city, a place where we could talk without fear of being overheard.

I arrived early, scanning the area for any signs of danger. Vortex appeared a few minutes later, a hooded figure with a confident stride. We exchanged brief pleasantries before getting down to business.

"I need information on the Shadow Collective," I said, my voice low. "Anything you can tell me about their operations, their members, their methods."

Vortex leaned against a tree, their expression thoughtful. "The Shadow Collective is no joke, AJ. They're highly organized and well-funded. Their leader, a hacker known as 'Wraith,' is one of the best in the business."

"Wraith?" I repeated, the name unfamiliar. "What else do you know about them?"

Vortex shrugged. "Not much. Wraith is a ghost, never seen, never heard. But their influence is everywhere. They have connections in high places, and they're always one step ahead."

It was a daunting prospect, but I was determined to learn more. "Can you help us track them down?"

Vortex hesitated for a moment before nodding. "I can try. But it won't be easy. The Shadow Collective is paranoid, and they cover their tracks well."

"Do whatever it takes," I said, my tone resolute. "We need to stop them."

With Vortex's help, we began to piece together a picture of the Shadow Collective's operations.

It was a slow and painstaking process, but each new piece of information brought us closer to understanding their network.

As we delved deeper, we discovered that the Shadow Collective had infiltrated several major corporations and government agencies. They had access to sensitive information and the means to cause significant damage.

One of their primary targets was a major financial institution, and the potential fallout from a successful attack was staggering.

We needed to act quickly to prevent it.

Agent Carter and Mike coordinated with the financial institution's security team to strengthen their defenses and prepare for a potential attack. It was a tense and uncertain time, but our preparations paid off.

When the Shadow Collective launched their attack, we were ready. Using the intelligence we had gathered, we were able to anticipate their moves and neutralize the threat.

It was a hard-fought victory, but it demonstrated the importance of our alliances and the value of our intelligence network.

But the fight was far from over. The Shadow Collective was still out there, and their determination to dominate the digital underworld was unwavering.

In the following months, we continued to work tirelessly to dismantle their network. It was a game of cat and mouse, with each side trying to outmaneuver the other.

But with each victory, we grew stronger, and our resolve deepened.

One of the key figures in our fight against the Shadow Collective was an ally we had gained during the Specter operation – a former hacker turned cyber security expert named Alex. Alex's knowledge and expertise were invaluable, and they quickly became an integral part of our team.

Together, we developed new strategies and tools to combat the Shadow Collective's attacks. It was a constant battle, but with each new challenge, we grew more confident in our ability to protect and defend against cyber threats.

But the fight against cybercrime was not without its sacrifices. The constant pressure and the ever-present danger took a toll on everyone involved. There were moments of doubt, moments when the weight of the mission seemed overwhelming.

But through it all, we remained united in our determination to make a difference. The alliances we had forged, the friendships we had built, and the victories we had achieved gave us the strength to continue.

As we faced new enemies and forged new alliances, one thing became clear – the fight against cybercrime was a never-ending battle. But as long as there were people willing to stand up and fight for justice, there was hope.

The road ahead was uncertain, filled with challenges and dangers. But we were ready to face it, knowing that we were stronger together and that our resolve was unbreakable.

The fight against the Shadow Collective had only just begun, and we were prepared to see it through to the end. Allies and enemies would come and go, but our commitment to justice would remain steadfast.

Chapter 7: The Deeper Conspiracy

With the Shadow Collective firmly in our sights, we intensified our efforts to dismantle their network. But as we dug deeper into their operations, it became clear that we were dealing with more than just a group of skilled hackers.

There was a deeper conspiracy at play, one that extended far beyond the digital realm.

The intelligence we had gathered revealed connections between the Shadow Collective and various powerful entities – corrupt officials, multinational corporations, and even rogue intelligence agents. It was a complex web of deceit and manipulation, and unraveling it would be no easy task.

Agent Carter, Mike, and I convened in the secure operations room, the walls lined with monitors displaying real-time data feeds and intelligence reports.

The atmosphere was tense, the weight of our discoveries pressing down on us.

"We're dealing with something much bigger than we initially thought," Agent Carter said, her voice steady but filled with concern. "The Shadow Collective is just one piece of a larger puzzle."

Mike nodded in agreement. "Their reach extends into places we never imagined.

We need to approach this carefully, or we risk exposing ourselves and jeopardizing the entire operation."

I leaned forward, my mind racing with possibilities. "We need to follow the money. These connections are fueled by financial interests. If we can trace the flow of funds, we might be able to identify the key players behind this conspiracy."

It was a daunting task, but it was our best shot at uncovering the truth.

We began to analyze financial transactions, looking for patterns and anomalies that could lead us to the masterminds behind the Shadow Collective.

As we delved deeper, we uncovered a series of shell companies and offshore accounts used to launder money and fund illegal activities. These financial entities were interconnected, forming a network that spanned multiple countries and jurisdictions.

One name kept appearing in our investigation – "Vanguard Holdings." It was a multinational conglomerate with interests in various industries, from finance to technology. On the surface, it appeared legitimate, but our analysis suggested otherwise.

"Vanguard Holdings is the key," I said, pointing to the data on the screen. "They're using their resources to fund the Shadow Collective and other criminal activities. We need to dig deeper into their operations."

Agent Carter nodded. "We'll need to coordinate with international partners to investigate Vanguard Holdings. This is going to be a delicate operation. We can't afford any mistakes."

We reached out to our allies, sharing our findings and coordinating efforts to investigate Vanguard Holdings. It was a complex and high-stakes operation, requiring cooperation and precision.

As we continued to gather intelligence, we discovered that Vanguard Holdings was involved in a wide range of illegal activities, from money laundering to corporate espionage. Their connections reached into the highest levels of government and business, making them a formidable adversary.

One of our key allies in the investigation was an intelligence officer named Elena. She had extensive experience in financial crimes and had been tracking Vanguard Holdings for years.

Her insights were invaluable, providing us with a clearer understanding of the conglomerate's operations.

"Vanguard Holdings operates like a shadow government," Elena explained during a secure video conference. "They have influence over politicians, control over major corporations, and the resources to manipulate markets. Taking them down won't be easy, but it's necessary."

With Elena's help, we began to map out a plan to expose Vanguard Holdings and bring their leaders to justice. It involved a multi-faceted approach, targeting their financial operations, uncovering their criminal activities, and building a case that could withstand legal scrutiny.

As we prepared for the operation, we faced numerous challenges and setbacks. Vanguard Holdings had layers of protection, both digital and physical, and their leaders were adept at covering their tracks.

But we pressed on, driven by our commitment to justice and the knowledge that we were making a difference. Each piece of evidence, each small victory, brought us closer to our goal.

One of the key breakthroughs came when we intercepted a series of encrypted communications between Vanguard Holdings and a high-ranking government official. The messages revealed plans to manipulate a major election, using their resources to influence the outcome and ensure their continued dominance.

"This is it," I said, my heart pounding as I read the messages. "This is the smoking gun we needed. We have to act fast."

Agent Carter and Mike agreed, and we immediately began to coordinate with our international partners to launch a series of simultaneous raids on Vanguard Holdings' facilities. It was a high-risk operation, but it was our best chance to dismantle their network and bring their leaders to justice.

The raids were executed with precision, and we managed to capture several key figures within Vanguard Holdings. The evidence we gathered was overwhelming, exposing the full extent of their criminal activities and their connections to the Shadow Collective.

As the dust settled, we knew that we had struck a significant blow against the conspiracy. Vanguard Holdings was crippled, and their leaders were facing justice. But we also knew that the fight was far from over.

The deeper conspiracy we had uncovered was vast and far-reaching, and there were still many questions left unanswered. But we were determined to see it through, to expose the truth and bring all those responsible to justice.

In the weeks that followed, we continued to unravel the web of deceit, working tirelessly to piece together the full picture. It was a challenging and often frustrating process, but we remained focused on our mission.

One of the most significant revelations came when we discovered a hidden archive of documents detailing the inner workings of Vanguard Holdings and their connections to various criminal organizations. It was a treasure trove of information, providing us with new leads and insights.

As we analyzed the documents, we realized that the conspiracy extended even further than we had initially thought. There were connections to other powerful entities, each one playing a role in the grand scheme.

"We're dealing with a Hydra," Elena said during a strategy meeting. "Cut off one head, and two more grow in its place. We need to be thorough and relentless."

Agent Carter agreed. "We have to stay vigilant and continue to build our network of allies. This fight is far from over, but we're making progress."

With renewed determination, we pressed on, knowing that the road ahead would be long and difficult.

But we were ready to face whatever challenges came our way, driven by our commitment to justice and the knowledge that we were making a difference.

The deeper conspiracy we had uncovered was a testament to the complexity and resilience of the forces we were up against. But it was also a reminder of the importance of our mission and the impact we could have.

Chapter 8: The Breaking Point

The deeper we delved into the conspiracy, the more we realized the enormity of the challenge before us. Each new revelation brought with it a sense of urgency, a reminder that our work was far from over.

But it also took a toll on everyone involved, testing our limits and pushing us to the breaking point.

The pressure was relentless. The Shadow Collective, though weakened, continued to mount attacks, their desperation driving them to take increasingly bold and dangerous actions. Vanguard Holdings, despite the capture of several key figures, still had significant resources at their disposal, and they were not about to go down without a fight.

Our team was stretched thin, juggling multiple investigations and operations simultaneously.

The constant threat of cyber attacks and the need to stay one step ahead of our adversaries left little room for rest or respite.

One evening, as I sat in the dimly lit operations room, my eyes fixed on the monitors displaying real-time data feeds, I felt the weight of exhaustion pressing down on me. The endless hours of work, the constant vigilance, and the ever-present danger were taking their toll.

Mike entered the room, a cup of coffee in hand. He handed it to me with a sympathetic smile. "You look like you could use this."

"Thanks," I said, gratefully accepting the coffee. "It's been a long few weeks."

Mike nodded, taking a seat next to me. "We're all feeling it. But we're making progress. We just have to keep pushing."

I appreciated his words of encouragement, but I couldn't shake the feeling of being overwhelmed. The stakes were higher than ever, and the margin for error was razor-thin.

As we continued to monitor the situation, a series of alerts flashed across the screens. Another cyber attack was underway, this time targeting a major hospital network. The implications were horrifying – patient records compromised, critical systems disrupted, lives at risk.

"We need to act fast," I said, my mind racing as I began to analyze the attack vectors. "We can't let this happen."

Agent Carter and the rest of the team quickly mobilized, coordinating with the hospital's IT staff to counter the attack and secure their systems. It was a tense and frantic effort, but we managed to neutralize the threat before any significant damage was done.

As the immediate crisis passed, the sense of relief was palpable, but so was the exhaustion. We had averted disaster, but it was a stark reminder of the constant danger we faced.

In the days that followed, we continued to face wave after wave of attacks. The Shadow Collective was relentless, their desperation driving them to take increasingly reckless actions. Each attack was a test of our resilience and determination.

But the constant pressure began to take its toll on the team. Tempers flared, mistakes were made, and the stress of the situation became increasingly apparent. We were all on edge, pushed to our limits.

One night, as I was working late in the lab, Agent Carter entered the room. She looked as tired as I felt, her eyes filled with concern.

"AJ, we need to talk," she said, taking a seat across from me.

I nodded, setting aside my work. "What's on your mind?"

"We're all feeling the strain," she said, her voice low and measured. "But I need you to take care of yourself. You're one of our best assets, and we can't afford to lose you."

I appreciated her concern, but I couldn't help but feel frustrated.

"I'm doing everything I can, Carter. But it's not enough. The attacks keep coming, and we're barely keeping our heads above water."

She sighed, her expression softening. "I know. But we have to find a way to push through. We can't let them win."

Her words resonated with me, a reminder of why we were doing this. The fight against cybercrime was more than just a job – it was a mission, a commitment to protect and defend.

As the days turned into weeks, we continued to face new challenges and setbacks. Each victory was hard-fought, each defeat a reminder of the stakes. But through it all, we remained determined to see it through.

One of the most significant breakthroughs came when we intercepted a series of encrypted communications between the Shadow Collective and a high-ranking official within Vanguard Holdings.

The messages revealed plans for a major cyber attack on a critical infrastructure target – a power grid that supplied electricity to millions of people.

"This is it," I said, my eyes fixed on the screen. "We can't let this happen."

Agent Carter and Mike immediately began to coordinate a response, working with local and federal agencies to secure the power grid and prevent the attack. It was a race against time, every second counting.

As the operation unfolded, the tension was palpable. The Shadow Collective's attack was sophisticated and well-coordinated, but our preparations paid off. We managed to neutralize the threat, averting what could have been a catastrophic disaster.

The victory was a significant one, but it also came at a cost. The constant pressure and the ever-present danger had taken their toll on the team. We were all exhausted, physically and mentally.

In the aftermath of the operation, we took a moment to regroup and reflect. The fight against cybercrime was far from over, but we had shown that we could stand our ground and protect what mattered most.

But as we prepared for the next phase of our mission, we knew that the breaking point was always looming. The constant pressure, the relentless attacks, and the high stakes would continue to test our limits.

We needed to find a way to balance our commitment to the mission with the need to take care of ourselves and each other. It was a delicate balance, but it was essential if we were to continue the fight.

Chapter 9: The Inside Man

 In the midst of our relentless fight against the Shadow Collective, we faced a new and unexpected challenge. It was a threat that came not from the outside, but from within.

 The discovery of an inside man within our ranks sent shockwaves through our team, shaking the foundation of trust and collaboration that we had built.

 The revelation came during a routine security audit.

Our systems had been compromised, sensitive information leaked, and operations jeopardized. The breach was sophisticated, executed with a level of precision that suggested an intimate knowledge of our protocols and defenses.

Agent Carter called an emergency meeting, her expression grim as she addressed the team. "We've identified a mole within our ranks," she said, her voice steady but filled with urgency.

"This individual has been feeding information to the Shadow Collective, compromising our operations and putting us all at risk."

The room fell silent, the weight of her words sinking in. Trust was the cornerstone of our team, and the realization that one of our own had betrayed us was a devastating blow.

"We need to identify the mole and neutralize the threat immediately," Mike said, his tone resolute. "Our mission depends on it."

The task of uncovering the inside man fell to me. Using my skills and knowledge of our systems, I began to trace the digital footprints left behind by the mole. It was a meticulous and painstaking process, but I was determined to get to the bottom of it.

As I delved deeper into the investigation, I uncovered a series of encrypted communications between the mole and the Shadow Collective.

The messages were carefully crafted, designed to avoid detection, but they revealed a pattern – the mole was passing along critical information about our operations, including plans for upcoming raids and intelligence reports.

The betrayal cut deep, but it also steeled my resolve. I worked tirelessly, following the digital breadcrumbs, analyzing logs, and cross-referencing data. Every lead brought me closer to identifying the mole.

One evening, as I was sifting through a particularly complex set of logs, I found a crucial piece of evidence – a series of login attempts that matched the mole's pattern. The timestamps and locations pointed to a specific individual within our team.

My heart pounded as I confirmed the identity of the mole. It was someone we had trusted, someone who had been with us from the beginning. The betrayal was personal, and it left a bitter taste in my mouth.

I immediately informed Agent Carter and Mike. Their expressions mirrored my own – a mix of anger, disbelief, and determination.

"We need to handle this carefully," Agent Carter said, her voice steady but filled with resolve. "We can't let the mole know we've discovered their identity. We need to gather more evidence and plan our approach."

We devised a plan to monitor the mole's activities, using their own tactics against them. We set up a series of traps, feeding them false information and tracking their communications with the Shadow Collective.

As the days passed, the evidence against the mole mounted. We documented their every move, compiling a comprehensive case that would hold up under scrutiny. It was a delicate balance, maintaining the facade of trust while working tirelessly behind the scenes to expose the truth.

Finally, the moment came to confront the mole. Agent Carter, Mike, and I gathered in a secure room, the atmosphere tense and charged with anticipation. The mole was brought in, their expression a mix of confusion and apprehension.

"What's going on?" they asked, their voice betraying a hint of nervousness.

"We know what you've been doing," Agent Carter said, her tone cold and unwavering.

"We've traced the leaks back to you. You've been feeding information to the Shadow Collective, compromising our operations and putting lives at risk."

The mole's face paled, their composure slipping. "I don't know what you're talking about," they stammered, their voice trembling.

"We have the evidence," I said, stepping forward. "Logs, communications, everything. You've betrayed us, and now you're going to face the consequences."

The mole's defiance crumbled, replaced by a look of defeat. "I had no choice," they said, their voice barely above a whisper. "They threatened my family. They said they would kill them if I didn't cooperate."

The revelation added a new layer of complexity to the situation. The mole's actions were driven by fear and coercion, a reminder of the ruthless tactics employed by the Shadow Collective.

"We'll ensure your family is protected," Agent Carter said, her tone softening slightly. "But you need to cooperate with us. Tell us everything you know."

The mole nodded, tears streaming down their face. "I'll tell you everything. Just please, protect my family."

With the mole's cooperation, we gained valuable insights into the Shadow Collective's operations and tactics. It was a breakthrough, but it also highlighted the lengths to which our enemies would go to achieve their goals.

As we moved forward, the sense of betrayal lingered, but it also strengthened our resolve. We were fighting a formidable enemy, one that was willing to use any means necessary to achieve their objectives.

The discovery of the inside man was a turning point, a reminder of the importance of vigilance and trust. It also underscored the complexity of our mission and the need to remain united in the face of adversity.

In the days that followed, we continued to dismantle the Shadow Collective's network, using the information provided by the mole to launch targeted operations and neutralize key threats. Each victory brought us closer to our goal, but it also reminded us of the challenges that lay ahead.

Chapter 10: Closing In

With the inside man neutralized and the Shadow Collective reeling from our recent victories, we intensified our efforts to dismantle their operations once and for all. The information provided by the mole had given us valuable insights into their network, and we were determined to use it to our advantage.

Our first priority was to target the remaining key figures within the Shadow Collective.

These individuals were the backbone of their operations, coordinating attacks, managing resources, and maintaining the flow of information. Without them, the organization would be crippled.

One of the most significant targets was a hacker known as "Cipher." Cipher was a master of encryption and a key player in the Shadow Collective's cyber attacks. Their skills were unparalleled, and their influence within the organization was substantial.

Using the intelligence we had gathered, we began to track Cipher's digital footprint. It was a complex and challenging task, but with each new piece of information, we got closer to pinpointing their location.

As we closed in on Cipher, we also uncovered a series of communications that revealed their next target – a major financial institution with global reach. The potential impact of a successful attack on this institution was staggering, and we knew we had to act quickly to prevent it.

Agent Carter, Mike, and I convened in the operations room, the atmosphere charged with urgency and determination. "We need to move fast," Agent Carter said, her voice steady but filled with resolve. "Cipher's planning an attack on the financial institution in less than 48 hours. We have to stop them."

Mike nodded in agreement. "We have the intel, but we need to be precise. One wrong move, and Cipher could slip through our fingers."

We formulated a plan to intercept Cipher and prevent the attack. It involved a coordinated effort between our team, the financial institution's security staff, and our international partners. The stakes were high, and failure was not an option.

As we prepared for the operation, I felt a mix of anticipation and apprehension. The fight against the Shadow Collective had been long and arduous, and this was a critical moment. We had to get it right.

On the day of the operation, we moved with precision and determination. Our team monitored Cipher's digital activities, tracking their movements and anticipating their next steps. The financial institution's security staff were on high alert, ready to respond to any signs of an attack.

As the clock ticked down, Cipher made their move. Using a series of sophisticated techniques, they attempted to breach the financial institution's defenses. But we were ready.

I worked tirelessly, countering Cipher's attacks and reinforcing the institution's security measures. It was a high-stakes digital battle, each side pushing the limits of their skills and resources.

Finally, we managed to trace Cipher's location to a remote facility in Eastern Europe. The digital trail led us to a small, unassuming building that served as their base of operations.

Agent Carter immediately coordinated with local law enforcement and our international partners to stage a raid on the facility. It was a high-risk operation, but it was our best chance to capture Cipher and prevent the attack.

The raid was executed with precision, the agents moving swiftly and silently. Inside the facility, they found Cipher and several associates, their equipment still active and displaying the ongoing attack.

Cipher attempted to resist, but they were quickly subdued. The facility was secured, and the attack on the financial institution was neutralized. It was a significant victory, a testament to our determination and teamwork.

Back at the lab, we analyzed the data recovered from Cipher's equipment. It provided us with valuable insights into the Shadow Collective's remaining operations and their connections to other criminal organizations.

As we continued to dismantle the Shadow Collective's network, we faced new challenges and obstacles. Each victory brought us closer to our goal, but it also highlighted the complexity and resilience of our adversaries.

One of the most significant discoveries came when we intercepted a series of communications between the Shadow Collective and a high-ranking official within a multinational corporation.

The messages revealed plans for a coordinated series of attacks on critical infrastructure targets around the world.

"This is bigger than we thought," Mike said, his expression grim as he reviewed the messages. "They're planning something massive, something that could cause widespread chaos."

Agent Carter nodded. "We need to act fast. We can't let them carry out these attacks."

We immediately began to coordinate with our international partners, sharing the intelligence and formulating a plan to prevent the attacks. It was a massive undertaking, requiring cooperation and coordination on a global scale.

As the operation unfolded, the tension was palpable. The Shadow Collective's attacks were sophisticated and well-coordinated, but our preparations paid off. We managed to neutralize the threats, preventing what could have been catastrophic disasters.

In the aftermath, we continued to dismantle the Shadow Collective's network, targeting their remaining key figures and disrupting their operations. Each victory was hard-fought, but it brought us closer to our goal.

The fight against the Shadow Collective had taken its toll, but it had also strengthened our resolve. We were more determined than ever to see it through, to bring justice to those who sought to sow chaos and destruction.

And with the support of our allies and the strength of our resolve, I knew that we could overcome any challenge and emerge victorious. The battle for the digital world was far from over, but we were prepared to fight, and we would never give up.

Chapter 11: The Final Showdown

The capture of Cipher and the prevention of the attacks on the financial institution and critical infrastructure were significant victories, but they were not the end of our fight against the Shadow Collective.

As we continued to dismantle their network, we knew that the final confrontation was imminent. The ultimate showdown with their leader, Wraith, was on the horizon.

Wraith was the elusive mastermind behind the Shadow Collective, a figure shrouded in mystery and fear. We had only fragments of information about them, but every lead we followed pointed to their central role in orchestrating the attacks and maintaining the network's cohesion.

Using the intelligence we had gathered, we began to narrow down Wraith's location. It was a painstaking process, involving the analysis of countless pieces of data, but each new piece brought us closer to our goal.

One of the most significant breakthroughs came when we intercepted a series of communications between Wraith and a high-ranking official within a powerful multinational corporation. The messages revealed plans for a final, decisive attack – one that would cripple global financial markets and cause widespread chaos.

"This is it," Agent Carter said, her voice filled with urgency. "We have to stop Wraith before they can carry out this attack. If they succeed, the consequences will be catastrophic."

Mike and I nodded in agreement. We knew that this was our chance to take down Wraith and dismantle the Shadow Collective once and for all.

We formulated a plan to intercept Wraith and prevent the attack. It involved a coordinated effort between our team, international law enforcement agencies, and private sector partners. The stakes were higher than ever, and failure was not an option.

As we prepared for the operation, the tension was palpable. We were facing our most formidable adversary, and the outcome of the showdown would determine the future of our fight against cybercrime.

The operation was set to take place in a remote location in Eastern Europe, where Wraith had established their base of operations. The facility was heavily fortified, and we knew that infiltrating it would be a challenging and dangerous task.

On the day of the operation, our team moved with precision and determination. The atmosphere was charged with anticipation as we prepared for the final confrontation.

I was stationed in the operations room, monitoring the situation through a secure feed. My heart pounded in my chest as I watched the live video streams from the agents' body cameras.

Agent Carter and Mike led the assault team, their expressions focused and resolute. The agents moved swiftly, breaching the facility with practiced ease. Inside, they encountered fierce resistance from Wraith's associates, but they pressed on, determined to reach their target.

As the battle raged on, I worked tirelessly to disable the facility's security systems and provide real-time intelligence to the assault team. It was a high-stakes digital battle, each side pushing the limits of their skills and resources.

Finally, the team reached the central command room, where Wraith was orchestrating the attack. The door was breached, and inside, they found Wraith – a figure clad in black, their face obscured by a mask.

"Hands up!" Agent Carter shouted, her weapon trained on Wraith.

Wraith turned, their eyes cold and calculating. "You think you can stop me?" they sneered. "You're too late."

But the team was prepared. They moved in swiftly, subduing Wraith and securing the facility. The attack was neutralized, and the Shadow Collective's network was crippled.

As Wraith was taken into custody, the sense of relief was overwhelming. We had done it – we had taken down the mastermind behind the Shadow Collective and prevented a catastrophic attack.

Back at the lab, we analyzed the data recovered from the facility. It provided us with valuable insights into the Shadow Collective's remaining operations and connections. With Wraith in custody, we were able to dismantle the remaining elements of the network and bring their associates to justice.

The final showdown had been a success, but it had come at a cost. The relentless pressure and the ever-present danger had taken their toll on the team.

We were exhausted, physically and mentally, but the sense of accomplishment was undeniable.

In the aftermath, we took a moment to reflect on our journey. The fight against the Shadow Collective had been long and arduous, filled with challenges and setbacks. But we had persevered, driven by our commitment to justice and our determination to make a difference.

As I looked out over the city, the lights flickering in the distance, I felt a sense of pride and fulfillment. The fight for justice was far from over, but we had achieved a significant victory. We had taken down one of the most formidable cybercriminal organizations in the world and brought their leader to justice.

But I also knew that the battle against cybercrime was never truly over. There would always be new threats, new challenges to face.

The digital world was constantly evolving, and we needed to remain vigilant and prepared.

As we celebrated our victory, we also began to plan for the future. We knew that we needed to continue to build our network of allies, to strengthen our defenses, and to stay one step ahead of those who sought to exploit the digital world for their gain.

The final showdown with Wraith had been a turning point, a testament to our resolve and our ability to overcome even the most formidable challenges.

But it was also a reminder of the importance of our mission and the impact we could have.

Chapter 12: Aftermath

The capture of Wraith and the dismantling of the Shadow Collective marked a significant milestone in our fight against cybercrime.

The sense of relief and accomplishment was palpable, but it also brought with it a moment of reflection. The journey had been long and arduous, filled with challenges and sacrifices, but we had emerged victorious.

In the days and weeks that followed, we focused on consolidating our gains and addressing the aftermath of the operation. The intelligence we had gathered provided us with valuable insights into the broader landscape of cybercrime, and we used this information to launch new initiatives and strengthen our defenses.

Agent Carter, Mike, and I worked tirelessly to ensure that the momentum we had gained was not lost.

We coordinated with our international partners, sharing our findings and collaborating on efforts to combat emerging threats. The spirit of cooperation and unity that had been forged during the fight against the Shadow Collective continued to drive our mission forward.

One of the most significant tasks was the prosecution of Wraith and their associates. The evidence we had gathered was overwhelming, and the legal process moved swiftly.

The trials were high-profile, drawing attention from around the world, and the sentences handed down sent a clear message – justice would be served.

But even as we celebrated our victories, we were acutely aware of the ongoing challenges. The fight against cybercrime was never-ending, and new threats were constantly emerging. We needed to remain vigilant and adaptive, ready to face whatever came next.

One of the most significant outcomes of our efforts was the establishment of a new international task force dedicated to combating cybercrime.

This task force brought together experts and resources from around the world, creating a united front against those who sought to exploit the digital world for their gain.

The task force was named the Global Cyber Defense Alliance (GCDA), and it quickly became a cornerstone of our efforts.

With its creation, we were able to streamline our operations, share intelligence more effectively, and coordinate responses to emerging threats.

As part of the GCDA, we launched several new initiatives aimed at strengthening our defenses and enhancing our capabilities.

These included advanced training programs for cyber security professionals, public awareness campaigns to educate individuals and businesses about the dangers of cybercrime, and cutting-edge research and development efforts to stay ahead of emerging threats.

The GCDA also fostered a spirit of collaboration and innovation, bringing together some of the brightest minds in the field to tackle the complex challenges of the digital age.

It was a testament to what we could achieve when we worked together, and it gave me hope for the future.

In the midst of these efforts, I also took some time to reflect on my personal journey.

The fight against the Shadow Collective had tested me in ways I had never imagined, pushing me to my limits and forcing me to confront my own fears and doubts. But it had also shown me the power of resilience and determination, and the importance of fighting for what was right.

As I looked back on the journey, I felt a sense of gratitude for the people who had stood by me – Agent Carter, Mike, Elena, Alex, and so many others.

Their support and dedication had been instrumental in our success, and I knew that we could not have achieved what we had without them.

The fight against cybercrime had brought us together, forging bonds that would last a lifetime.

It had shown us the importance of unity and collaboration, and it had reminded us of the impact that we could have when we worked together towards a common goal.

As we moved forward, I knew that the challenges would continue, but I also knew that we were ready to face them. The lessons we had learned, the victories we had achieved, and the bonds we had forged would guide us as we navigated the complex and ever-changing landscape of the digital world.

Epilogue: A New Dawn

The dust had settled, and the city was beginning to return to a sense of normalcy. The lights of Philadelphia flickered like a constellation of resilience and hope, each one a testament to the strength and determination of its people. As I walked through the bustling streets, I couldn't help but feel a sense of pride and accomplishment.

The fight against the Shadow Collective had been long and arduous, but we had emerged victorious.

The capture of Wraith and the dismantling of their network marked a significant milestone in our mission to combat cybercrime, but it was also a reminder of the ongoing challenges we faced.

The creation of the Global Cyber Defense Alliance (GCDA) had been a pivotal moment, bringing together resources and expertise from around the world to create a united front against cyber threats.

It was a testament to what we could achieve when we worked together, and it gave me hope for the future.

As I made my way to a small café in Center City, I thought about the journey that had brought me here. From my early days as a hacker navigating the digital world to my role as a key player in the fight against cybercrime, it had been a path filled with twists and turns, challenges and triumphs.

I entered the café and spotted Agent Carter and Mike sitting at a corner table. They waved me over, their expressions warm and welcoming. As I joined them, we exchanged smiles and settled into a comfortable conversation.

"We did it," Agent Carter said, her voice filled with pride. "We took down the Shadow Collective and brought Wraith to justice."

Mike nodded in agreement. "It was a team effort. We couldn't have done it without everyone's dedication and hard work."

I smiled, feeling a sense of camaraderie and gratitude. "We've come a long way, but there's still so much to do. The fight against cybercrime is never-ending, but we're ready to face whatever comes next."

As we talked, I couldn't help but think about the future. The digital world was constantly evolving, and new threats were always emerging. But with the support of our allies and the strength of our resolve, I knew that we could overcome any challenge.

The establishment of the GCDA had created a solid foundation for our efforts, and I was confident that we would continue to make progress in the fight against cybercrime. The bonds we had forged, the lessons we had learned, and the victories we had achieved would guide us as we navigated the complex landscape of the digital age.

As our conversation continued, we were joined by Elena and Alex, their faces reflecting the same sense of accomplishment and determination.

We talked about our plans for the future, the initiatives we were launching, and the challenges we anticipated.

It was a moment of reflection and celebration, but it was also a reminder of the work that lay ahead. The fight for justice was far from over, but we were ready to face whatever came next.

As I left the café and walked through the streets of Philadelphia, I felt a renewed sense of purpose and hope.

The city was a symbol of resilience and strength, and it was a reminder of why we fought so hard to protect and defend.

The lights of the city flickered like beacons of hope, guiding us forward as we continued our mission. The fight against cybercrime was never-ending, but we were ready to face the challenges with determination and resolve.

As I looked out over the city, I felt a sense of pride and fulfillment. The journey had been long and challenging, but it had also been rewarding and transformative. We had made a difference, and we would continue to do so.

www.ingramcontent.com/pod-product-compliance
Lightning Source LLC
LaVergne TN
LVHW051231050326
832903LV00028B/2347